What's Inside

PRIME TIME FAMILY SERIES

DONNA ERICKSON'S
Travel
FUN BOOK

Illustrated by David LaRochelle

Augsburg

MINNEAPOLIS

To my friend Becky Anderson,
who shared my first grand travel adventure—
when Europe was $5 a day.

Cover design by David Meyer
Cover photograph by Ann Marsden

ISBN 0-8066-3337-9
Printed in the U.S.A.

Notes from Donna

Travel: A Family Adventure

Over the past few years, my family has made a tradition of spending a week together in the great outdoors. Our trek takes us to the Boundary Waters Canoe Area, a beautiful  natural treasure of protected woods and lakes along the border between Minnesota and Ontario, Canada. We leave behind the TV, the telephone, and even Minnesota Twins baseball games.

So what do we do that lures us away? Quite simply, for most of the time we sit in a fishing boat. We may fly in all directions 51 weeks of the year, but for seven days we are contained. We can't escape one another. We swat mosquitoes, tell silly jokes, and snag lines. And we talk. Our spirits are lifted by fresh air and the thrill of spotting a bear cub in a tree or gulls perched on mossy rocks.

Getting off the fast track isn't as easy for families as it used to be. Now, more than ever, we must be intentional about slowing down, saying no to busyness when it crowds in and threatens to disrupt plans for time together.

With careful planning and prioritizing, a trip can be a time to show we care and to nurture what is most precious to us—our children.

This book is filled with ideas to help you make the most of your family trip: tips for group planning that will help ensure a good time, suggestions for things to do and see on the way, creative ideas for filling the days once you've arrived, and thoughts about how you can extend and relive your trip back home. Plus, there's a whole section on minitrips that can turn a day outing into a family-building experience you'll treasure for years.

*Remember ...
it's the little
things that count.*

Donna Erickson

Get Ready, Get Set...

Preparing for Big Trips

Vacations are special times for families. To make them extra special, include the entire family in the planning and preparations. Here are some tips for pre-travel planning.

• Arriving unprepared in a new city or country can be intimidating to children—and to adults. Check out books, pamphlets, and magazines from your local library, and spend time together learning about your destination. Pinpoint particular landmarks or attractions that will be of special interest to children.

• Children may write to the chamber of commerce or tourist bureau of the place you will be visiting. Encourage them to ask for information of particular interest, such as attractions they might enjoy and special events that might be taking place during your visit. Children love receiving their own "travel" mail. If you have access to the Internet, search for up-to-date tourist, travel, and weather information.

• Before traveling to a country where English is not spoken, check out language tapes from the library or enroll in language classes offered in your community. (Many schools and community centers offer classes for children.) Concentrate on learning useful phrases.

• Children will enjoy handling their own money for special gift purchases, postcards, and stamps. This encourages personal financial responsibility, and the kids may also improve their math skills in the process. Identification and valuables can be carried in a small pouch or purse attached to the child's belt or hung around the neck.

• Your children can have fun helping pack for the trip. Personal items they choose to take will be of comfort to them in an unfamiliar place.

As you plan with your children, share their enthusiasm and excitement, anticipate their questions, and—once on your way—take many pictures to capture the memories.

Flying—with Kids

Finding vacation dates that jibe with work schedules, holiday breaks, and school and sports programs can be daunting. Today's busy families may need to opt for long-weekend vacations; and less time away often means traveling by plane. Here are some practical tips for high-flying families.

• Whenever possible, book nonstop flights. If a layover or change of plane is necessary and you find yourself with extra time in an airport, ask about designated play areas for kids.

• When two adults travel with young children, teamwork is the key to enjoying the trip. One adult can board with kiddie paraphernalia and get it stowed Meanwhile, the children can let their wiggles out in the terminal and board later with the other adult.

• Let your kids pack their own backpacks to carry on the plane. With the limited space on board, they'll have to pick and choose carefully. Double-check to be sure your child's security blanket or stuffed animal is tucked in.

• Bring along surprises for kids in your own tote bag. For a great "messless" activity, pick up inexpensive "magic paint" watercolor books, small paintbrushes or cotton swabs. Kids can dip these into water cups on their tray tables and apply water to the pages. Color will magically appear.

• Ask a flight attendant if the airline provides complementary stationery and envelopes. School-age children enjoy writing to relatives and friends on official airline paper.

• If you need to order special kids' meals for the flight, call the airline at lest 24 hours in advance. Menus will vary, and may include peanut butter sandwiches, pizza or hamburgers, with fruit and cookies.

Hotel & Motel Tips

If your vacation plans include stays in hotels or motels, you'll benefit from advanced planning and a few common-sense precautions once you've checked in.

• Be sure to book your room as soon as possible. Rates frequently can be negotiated over the phone. Ask about special promotions, coupons, and weekend family rates, as well as discounts for senior citizens and military personnel. And be sure to ask if there is a pool, a real plus after a tiring day on the road.

• Bring along a night-light to use in the room. And never leave home without your child's security blanket or favorite cuddly toy.

• If you're traveling with a toddler, take a few minutes to childproof the room upon arrival. For example, hang a towel over the top of an open bathroom door. If your child wanders into the bathroom and tries to close the door, he or she won't accidentally be locked inside.

• To save money and time, eat a simple breakfast in your room before heading out for the day. Serve cereal, milk (keep cool overnight in an ice-filled sink covered with layers of newspaper), and juice or fruit.

For a clever breakfast-on-the-road, serve cereal and milk in a scooped-out cantaloupe half. A unique bowl of fruit with cereal!

Map It Out Together

Here's a pre-trip strategy that everyone can enjoy and benefit from. Gather the whole family around a road map of the area you'll cover on your trip. Use a marker or colored pen to highlight the highways and side roads you plan to take. Talk about cities and towns you'll pass through. The children will have fun estimating distances and then checking their guesses against the key on the map.

Discuss special landmarks you may wish to visit. And, if there's time, children might want to do some research to explore cities, sights, and historical landmarks you'll pass along the way.

Preschoolers will feel part of the decision making when they are involved in these planning stages. And your older children will enjoy reinforcing the geography skills they are learning in school.

Keep the map handy once you're on the road. Children can take turns being navigators or tour guides as they consult information highlighted on the map.

Keeping in Touch
When Adults Travel

You will need: 4" x 6" index cards (one for each
                child for each day you are gone)

It's not uncommon nowadays for Mom and Dad
to take a trip without the kids. Parents may accompany each other on a business trip, take off to a foreign country for a number of days, or just have a
weekend getaway together. To involve the kids
and keep them aware of your travel plans, try this
activity. It really works—and best of all, it encourages exchanges of experiences once the trip is over
and you are back home.

On one side of an index card, print the date of
your first day away, and briefly state what you
intend to do. Add a personal comment if you wish.
For example:

> I arrive in Brussels today. I love their french fries.
> The Belgians eat french fries with mayonnaise.
> Isn't that funny?

Make a similar card for each day you will be
gone. Instruct the person who is caring for your
children to give them a card to read each day at
breakfast. In the evening the children may write
about their day on the backside of their card.
(Children who are too young to write can dictate
to an older sibling or adult.)

When you return from your trip, sit down with
your kids and read through the cards. You can
catch up on what you missed while gone, and they
can relive your vacation!

Hit the Road!

Good Times in the Car

If you're traveling a long distance by car, here are some ways to make sure it's a pleasant trip—and not a backseat nightmare.

• Once you hit the road, make frequent rest stops. Everyone needs a stretch and a break from the close quarters inside the car. When kids get fidgety and tempers flare, a change of scenery works wonders. Bring along fun equipment for exercise: jump ropes, bubble solution and a wand, and balls.

• Here's a way to keep school-age youngsters entertained while encouraging good reading habits. Clip and set aside articles and stories that appeal to your children's interests. For example, save a magazine story about a baseball player your child admires, a review of a film your child wants to see, or cartoons that will tickle your child's funny bone. Pack these in the car for special quiet-time reading.

• To help keep dispositions on an even keel, have healthy snacks on hand. Kids enjoy picking out raisins, fruit snacks, and cereal from small plastic margarine containers they can store in their backpacks. Replenish snacks when needed. A plastic sports bottle with attached straw is perfect for beverages.

• If your car has a tape deck, check out audio cassettes of favorite children's books from your local library. Once each morning and afternoon, play a portion of a story, stopping at an exciting point (a "cliffhanger"). Kids will eagerly look forward to each next installment.

• Catch your kids doing something good. Complimenting them for appropriate and reasonably good behavior will go a long way to promote a cooperative spirit in the car.

Mileage Countdown Bags

You will need: 3 or 4 paper lunch bags
for each child
string or ribbon
felt-tipped markers
inexpensive toys that can
be used in the car:
books, stickers, etc.
snack items: small packages
of peanuts, raisins,
granola bars, rice cakes,
boxes of fruit juice, etc.
jump rope (for a rest stop)

Even though this activity requires extra effort on the part of Mom or Dad, it will be worth it once you are on the road. Not only does it curb the whining question, "Are we almost there?", but it also encourages good behavior as kids anticipate opening their next mileage bag. Older children will be able to trace your route on the map and predict when the mileage bag will come.

Before your trip, allocate three or four lunch bags for each child. Looking at your planned route on the map, determine points where you think the kids will be ready for a snack, toy, game, book, etc. Every 50 miles or so seems to work best for school-age children. Write the number of miles you have traveled or the name of the city you will arrive at on each bag. Children will receive the appropriate bag at the spot you have noted.

Put an item in each bag, making sure that each child receives the same type of treat at the same time. For example, put one juice box in each 100-mile bag. Try to judge when certain items would be appropriate and helpful.

Tie the bags shut with string or ribbon, and place them in a basket or box that will sit next to you during the trip. Explain the mileage game at the beginning of the trip, and watch the miles fly by!

Alphabet Diary Game

You will need: a small 50-page notebook
a large zipper-style style
plastic bag
a pen or pencil
crayons or felt-tipped markers
(optional)

Here's an activity that will keep your children occupied in the car, because they will be busy looking for interesting things en route.

Before you leave, the children can use fancy, colorful lettering to write their names, the date of departure, and your destination on the cover of their notebooks. Then, at the top of each page, they can print one letter of the alphabet, beginning with A and ending with Z. (An older sibling or Mom or Dad could help younger children.) Store the notebook and pencil in the plastic bag.

On the road, the children can be on the lookout for special landmarks or items of interest. They can write the names of what they see next to the appropriate letters in their notebooks, and then draw a picture of the item under each word. For example, the word *barn* and a picture of a barn would go on the page with B at the top.

After reaching your destination, encourage the children to continue filling in the blank pages. Extra pages can serve as a diary of activities you and your family take part in during the rest of your vacation. Once home, the entire family will enjoy looking at one another's ABC diaries, now and in years to come.

Auto Magnetism

You will need: magnetic-backed letters, num-
bers, and toys that you have
around the house
stainless-steel cookie sheet or
cake pan with lid that magnets stick to
zipper-style plastic bag
self-adhesive-backed magnetic
strips (optional)

Gather all the magnetic-backed toys your
kids play with, including those on your refrig-
erator door, or create some of your own by
attaching self-stick magnets to the backs of
small toys. Store them in the cake plan or plastic bag. Once on your way, your child can spell
words or create pictures on the cookie sheet or
cake pan with the magnets.

For older children, you may want to pur-
chase small travel game sets, such as checkers
or chess, that have magnetic-backed pieces for
easy playing in the car.

Pockets of Fun

Whether you're driving across town to visit grandparents or across the country for a once-in-a lifetime trip, here are ideas for keeping the car organized and the kids happily busy.

• Corral travel toys and treats in an inexpensive shoe organizer with pockets. Stitch lengths of elastic or ribbon to the corners of the organizer and attach it to the backside of the front car seat. Once it's firmly in place, fill the pouches with surprises for each young traveler: games, hand puppets, audio cassettes, favorite books, toy cars and trucks, stuffed animals, lacing and counting activities, pencils and markers, small tablets, snacks, etc.

• For toddlers, pick up a package of interlocking plastic links. Hook three or four links together, attach a toy to one end and link the other end to your child's car seat. If the toy drops, it won't fall on the floor. Attach a bagel to another string of links for a messless snack your young traveler will enjoy.

TIE AROUND
BACK OF
FRONT
SEAT

"Going to the Moon" in a Car

This car game has become our family favorite because all ages can play it together. Best of all, kids won't get carsick craning their necks hunting for words on road signs and license plates, or get dizzy looking for lost pieces from their car bingo game.

My daughter taught us to play "Going to the Moon" on a trip to beautiful Breckenridge, Colorado. It got us though snowstorms, slippery mountain roads, and being asked too many times, "Are we there yet?"

Here's how to play.

The person who is IT thinks of three things that have something in common. For example, the items might be a mango, a pineapple, and a papaya (all of them are

tropical fruits). The person who is IT then says to the other players, "I'm going to the moon and taking a mango, a pineapple, and a papaya. Who wants to come with me?" Given the clues, the first player tries to figure out what the items have in common and then thinks of a fourth item. If that person says, "banana," for example, the person who is IT responds by saying, "You may come with me." Then the next player names another item. (If a player states an item that doesn't fit, he or she may try again on the next turn.) When someone correctly guesses what all three items have in common, the round is over.

Game topics can be as simple or as complicated as you choose. Try to accommodate even the youngest in the family when playing "Going to the Moon."

When You Get There...

Do-It-Yourself Postcards

You will need: 1 zipper-style plastic bag
       or tote bag
     crayons
     stickers
     felt-tip markers
     pre-stamped, blank postcards
       from the post office

Here's an idea that doesn't require a lot of packing space, and the activity will keep kids happily busy during idle time away from home.

Fill a bag with art supplies and blank, pre-stamped postcards that you've addressed with names of relatives and children's friends.

During your trip—on the plane, in the car, in the hotel, on a park bench—children can turn these postcards into day-by-day pictures of their experiences. Encourage them to draw scenes of places you visit and people you see. When the drawing is complete, your child can write a message on the other side (or dictate one to a parent) and then drop the card in the mail.

Snapshots on Tape

You will need: portable tape recorder
blank cassette tapes

To add a new and lasting dimension to your trip, capture it on tape. Take turns with your kids being roving reporters who provide an exciting travelogue of the family vacation.

Begin the tape when you set out. Tell who will be "reporting," where you are going, what stops you plan to make, what each person is especially looking forward to. Then, as you visit historic landmarks, spots of beauty, or bustling cities, pass the tape recorder around so everyone can offer a personal description and reaction to the scene. Include accounts of your favorite meals, your hotel accommodations, most humorous experiences, etc. (Be sure to identify the place and the date of each entry.)

With your assistance, older children may also enjoy interviewing people they meet along the way: a forest ranger, waiter, flight attendant, or tour guide.

Label and store each tape after you've filled it. When you're back at home, gather around the tape recorder for an evening of delightful reminiscing and laughs.

Family Voices from Afar

You will need: a tape recorder or video camera
a blank cassette or videotape

Preserve a bit of family history as you collect voices from far-flung family members at a family reunion. This is a fun activity for visits to distant relatives or at a family reunion.

A bonus to this activity is the relationships that develop between children and older adults. Children can pretend they are reporters and prepare questions in advance.

Here are some idea-starters:

- What is your birth date?
- Where were you born?
- What were your parents' and grand-parents' names?
- What did they do for a living?
- What special thing do you remember about them?

- Where did you go to school?
- What did you like most or least about school?
- Describe the house (or town) you grew up in.
- Have you ever been married?
- How did you meet your spouse?
- Describe your first date.
- How long have you lived in this house (or town)?
- What do you like best about this part of the country?
- What has changed most in your lifetime?

At the beginning of the interview, record the date, location, and names of the people. Once you start asking questions, let the conversation develop on its own. You'll be learning exciting things about different parts of the country as you capture wonderful fragments of family history.

Postcard Travel Journal

You will need: postcards (collected as you visit
different places)
paper punch
metal ring (found at stationery
stores)

Keeping a travel diary can be unrealistic for
many young children, especially after a tiring
day of travel. An easy way to keep a record of
the day's activities and places visited is to collect picture postcards as the trip progresses.
When the children have a few quiet moments
after lunch, for example, they can jot down on
the backside of the postcard the date and what
they did at the place pictured. As they collect
the postcards, punch a hole in the top left cor-
ner and attach them together on a metal ring.
The kids will enjoy looking through the postcards and reading their notes months after
the trip.

CALIFORNIA!

GOLDEN GATE BRIDGE

POSTCARD

We rode a
cable car like
this one today.
It was exciting
(and a little scary!)

Junior Tour Guides

If your trip includes a visit to a big city, here's an activity that will take your family to exciting sites while helping your kids learn to read a map and street signs, and follow directions. (This activity can be adapted for suburban or rural families that want to spend a day or weekend in the city.)

Before you go, write or call the local Chamber of Commerce or Tourist Information Center, requesting a "walking tour map." Many cities now have a toll-free 800 number you can use to order brochures, maps, and transportation schedules. Or check out the possibility of getting a city map off the Internet.

Sit down together with the map and plan your family tour. List sights everyone wants to see, such as zoos, museums, aquariums, parks, and exhibits. Decide if you will hunt down destinations by foot, subway, bus, train, or even cable car. Then mark your route on the map.

With the list and marked map in hand, the kids can be your official guides. Encourage them to follow the map, ask questions if necessary, and check off signs at each destination. They'll enjoy reading the names of stations and terminals, and calculating appropriate fares.

As your junior tour guides lead you on their chosen routes, they will reinforce their reading skills and sharpen their sense of direction—and they'll get excellent math practice by counting coins and tokens.

Back Home Again

Trip Memory Collage

You will need: favorite vacation souvenirs and "finds," such as ticket stubs, postcards, travel brochures, maps, snapshots, etc.
18" x 24" poster frame (available at discount stores)
construction paper or posterboard, cut to size of frame
glue or adhesive putty (available at office supply and art stores)

Whether it's shells from the beach, ticket stubs from museums and ball games, picture postcards, or restaurant menus, we all love to collect vacation souvenirs. Here's an easy way to put those memories on display instead of letting them collect dust.

Place the poster frame on a flat surface and remove the clips and glass. Wash the glass and set it aside. Place the construction paper or poster board on the frame backing. Arrange the souvenir items—several "favorites" from each family member—fixing them to the paper with a dot of glue or putty. When complete, place glass over the collage and attach metal clips. Hang the finished collage in the kitchen or family room, where everyone can recall the good times together. And because the frame snaps apart, you can reuse it year after year, replacing old memories with new ones.

A Vacation Read-Aloud Book

You will need: vacation souvenirs, such as brochures,
ticket stubs, postcards, photos, and
other "finds"
tape recorder and blank cassettes
large sheet of art paper or construction
paper
felt-tipped markers or crayons
glue or tape
ribbon or yarn
paper punch

Foster your children's interest in books and reading
while helping them preserve highlights of the family
trip. With this project, even kids who are too young to
read can make their own storybooks.

Set out souvenirs that your children collected from
the family trip and help them organize the items:
outdoor sights and activities, museum visits, hotels
and restaurants—whatever groupings you choose.
Children can glue or tape each grouping onto a sheet
of art or construction paper, and then label the page.

Next, get out the tape recorder and encourage the
children to tell a story about the trip, mentioning each
souvenir and what they remember about that part of
the trip. You can operate the "record" button, stopping
when necessary for kids to collect their thoughts. After
one grouping has been covered, add a pause before
moving on to the next "page."

When you've finished recording, children might
enjoy adding their own drawings of vacation sights to
the pages of souvenirs. Punch holes in the sheets of
paper and tie them together with ribbon or yarn to
complete the book.

Souvenir See-Through Pouches

You will need: 6" wide fusible transparent
plastic ribbon (inexpensive and
available by the foot at craft
stores)
iron, or electric hair-curling iron
leather lacing, ribbon, or cording
souvenir nature finds, such as
beach shells, pebbles, miniature
pinecones, pressed leaves, small
feathers, etc.

When you've returned from an outdoor family
vacation or camping trip, the kids will have fun
making special see-through pouches to show off
their collection of souvenirs. The pouches can be
threaded onto a piece of leather lacing to create a
souvenir necklace that both boys and girls will
enjoy wearing.

Cut a 2" x 4" piece of plastic (smaller, if you
wish). Fold the plastic in half. An adult should use
a curling iron or medium-hot iron to seal together
the side and bottom edges of the plastic. After it
has cooled for several minutes, drop a nature find
into the pouch and seal the top closed. When it is
cool, punch a small hole through the top. Thread
as many pouches as you like onto leather lacing,
ribbon, or cording. Knot, and it's ready to wear.

Use this technique to display other small vacation souvenirs as well: ticket stubs, coins from
other countries, bus or subway tokens, buttons
and pins. Your children will have portable show-
and-tell displays for school and wonderful wear-
able reminders of great vacation times.

A Hanging Scrapbook

You will need: a length of clothesline or rope
clothespins or colorful art clips
colored markers
"hangable" vacation souvenirs:
pennants, T-shirts, posters,
brochures, concert or sports
programs, postcards,
maps, etc.

Here is an easy way to add a touch of fun
and family memories to the decor of your
child's room. String a clothesline from one
wall to another in the room. Decorate wooden
clothespins with markers, or use art clips to
hang favorite vacation mementos.

This "line of memories" makes an eye-catch-
ing display and, as the school year progresses,
souvenirs can be replaced with classroom
projects, party invitations, awards, and sports
memorabilia.

A Sticks and Stones and Shells Display

You will need: a clear glass vase with a base
at least 3" in diameter
rocks or shells about 1" to 1½"
in diameter
dried weeds or flowers

Do seashells from the beach turn up in the strangest places around your home? Consider putting your favorites on display in this attractive and contained fashion.

Place rocks or shells into the vase until they fill about ⅓ of the container. If you and your child have "finds" from a nature walk (such as dried weeks, flowers, or cattails) arrange them in the vase, too.

Set the arrangement on a table, mantel, or hutch—wherever it will get the most attention. Children will enjoy pointing out their favorite rocks and telling stories about where they collected the shells or picked the weeds.

If you wish, add some water in the vase, place a candle nearby, and make it the centerpiece of your dinner table. The collected "gems" will sparkle.

WILSON FAMILY
TRAVEL EXHIBIT

Travel Discovery Nook

You will need: a shelf or small table in your
family room or kitchen
index cards
pens or felt-tipped markers
souvenirs and "found" objects
from your family trips

SEAGULL FEATHER

Set aside a spot in your family room or kitchen to showcase mementos from the big trip. Your own "travel museum" can provide a hands-on travelogue for visitors to your home. Kids will love being museum guides, describing where each item comes from and how it featured in the family trip. Best of all, the collection will be a constant reminder of the time you spent together, discovering the excitement and beauty of faraway places.

For extra fun, label the souvenirs with small strips of index cards similar to those labels you see in museums. Describe the item, and tell where it came from and how you acquired it. For example:

This piece of driftwood comes from the beach at Ocean City, Maryland. Jill found it at 6:30 in the morning of June 30, after a stormy night. We think it is oak.

If your family travels to a new places each year, add items to the table in attractive ways. Trips to different beaches can be remembered by layering sand from each beach in a clear recycled jar. It's fun to see the range of colors and types of sand from one spot to another. And it's a unique way to recall a November trip to Clearwater Beach, Florida, and a July visit to Santa Cruz, California.

Day Trips
Around Town

Farmer's Market Food and Fun

From late spring until well into autumn, there's nothing like a weekend outing to a local farmers' market for wonderful sights, smells, and tastes of the season. No matter when you visit, you'll find luscious home-grown fruits and vegetables, and a host of other mouthwatering treats. Try to get an early start: the best produce is often gone by noon. Bring along empty bags and baskets—one for each family member—and make one walk-through just to see what's there.

Then take your time selecting ingredients for hearty soups, fresh salads, and home-baked pies and cobblers. Children will enjoy and learn from conversations with the farmers who grow the produce.

Once you're back home, consider the following ideas for enjoying the crops you've "harvested."

• Make a big pot of hearty vegetable soup. Kids can help with the scrubbing and chopping. Or introduce your family to eggplant in a dish of ratatouille.

• Toss up a colorful confetti salad: shredded lettuce; diced cucumbers, tomatoes, and red and green peppers; and chopped green onions.

• Decorate your home by tying bunches of large chili peppers together at the stems with raffia or twine. Make a loop at the top for a hanger. Make several bunches, add ribbons, hang to dry, and then share them with friends.

Family Fishing

It didn't take much to get my kids hooked on fishing when they were young. Ever since, one of our favorite family outings is still a day of fishing, topped off with a picnic supper.

If your kids are tipping the scales in favor of fishing for summer fun, there are two ideas for expanding the day into a super family experience.

When the fish don't bite.

Don't be surprised if younger kids get bored easily. For extra fun, join them in skipping stones along the shoreline or help them create a natural centerpiece for the picnic table. Scoop wet sand in an empty aluminum pie tin. Arrange shells, pebbles, pieces of bark, driftwood, and other finds on the damp sand. At mealtime, place a votive candle or two in the arrangement for an adult to light. The whole family will enjoy the lovely, glowing souvenir of the day.

Something fishy to end the day.

At nighttime, gather everyone together around a campfire or at a cozy place back home and tell a big fish tale, round-robin style. Ask a volunteer to start with a few sentences, then another person continues. Let everyone contribute to the story in an imaginative way using songs, gestures, or sound effects.

Berry Picking

Nothing beats the simple pleasure of taking a trip in the country to pick sweet, ripe strawberries and raspberries. Here are some tips and ideas for enjoying a favorite healthy treat.

Before you leave:

• Make a special berry-picking container for your preschooler by cutting several holes the size of a half dollar in the lid of a gallon-size plastic ice-cream bucket. Sand around the edges to make the holes smooth. Then snap the lid on the empty bucket. As the young berry-pickers harvest their berries, they can drop them through the holes. The berries won't fall out if the bucket tips over.
• Call to verify that the farm is open and that the fruit you are seeking is available. Ask for directions to the farm and be sure to check if children are welcome.
• Wear comfortable clothes and bring along sunglasses, sunscreen, hats for the whole family, and snacks for a picnic lunch.

When you return:

• Hulling strawberries is easy if you push a plastic straw through the pointed end of the strawberry all the way to the opposite end. The leafy stem will pop out and you won't waste any of the fruit in the process.
• For a quick and easy gourmet snack, put a strawberry on a toothpick and dip half of the strawberry into melted chocolate. Place the berry on waxed paper to dry. Make a number of these and serve.

Bring Home the Beach

You will need: 1 box of plaster of paris
(available from paint and hardware stores)
coffee can or plastic ice-cream pail
paint-stirring sticks
paper cup
paper clips

Bring along a carton of plaster of paris, a paper cup, and a coffee can the next time you go to the beach, and come home with a unique piece of art. If your kids have made plaster handprints in school, they'll be familiar with the "how-to"s.

Scoop out a design at least 2" deep in the wet sand. (Be sure the tide won't be coming in soon!) Connecting areas should also be 2" wide, to keep your project from breaking. This will be your mold. Decorate it with natural

objects you collect on the beach, including shells, rocks, sticks, bark, or weeds. When your mold is complete, mix the plaster of paris. Pour one or two cups of lake or sea water into the coffee can or pail. Add the powdered plaster and stir. The mixture should be smooth and thick—the consistency of a milk shake. Immediately pour the mixture into your sand mold, spreading it evenly to all areas with a stick, if necessary.

To make a hanger for your project, poke a paper clip halfway into the plaster at the center top. If the project is large, you may wish to position two paper clips evenly spaced from each side.

Allow the plaster to harden (1 to 1½ hours, depending on the size of the project), and then carefully remove the plaster souvenir from the sand. Dispose of the leftover plaster coffee can properly. Take a picture of your pleased kids holding their creations before you transport them home.

MOLD
SCOOPED
OUT OF →
SAND

Dream Vacations for Mom or Dad

Treat Mom or Dad to an exotic trip without ever leaving home. Kids will enjoy "traveling along" as they gather props and act as tour guides.

Make a "passport" with Mom or Dad's picture inside. Next, create a skit in which everyone plays a role on the airplane en route to the destination. While the pilot describes points of interest "below," a flight attendant can serve sparking juice—in the first-class cabin, of course.

• **Trip to the Caribbean.** In a sunny room, set out a beach chair with towels, sandals, and suntan lotion. Blow up colorful beach balls and hang them from the ceiling. Scatter shells on the floor. Play tapes of waves crashing, steel drums, or Beach Boys tunes. Offer fruit slushes or a fruit salad for a snack.

• **Trip to Africa.** Rent a safari video or the movie *The African Queen*. Snack on peanuts in the shell and tropical fruit on skewers. As a "souvenir," give a book on protecting endangered species. Or visit the zoo and look for African animals.

• **Trip to Paris.** Draw a mural of the Eiffel Tower on butcher paper and hang it on the wall. Hunt through the dress-up box to create a fashion show. "French waiters" in berets can serve café au lait, croissants, French cheese, or omelettes. Later, visit an art museum and look for paintings by French artists.

Trips Near and Far—in Books

One of the most exciting—and easiest—ways to travel to distant and exotic lands is through books. A whole world awaits your family on the shelves of your local library. Here are some simple and creative ideas to help open your child's mind to other lands and cultures.

• Make a list with your child of storybook characters from other parts of the world. For example, your family may be familiar with Madeline from France, Anansi from Africa, Pippi Longstocking from Sweden, and Ping from China. Spend time revisiting these delightful characters, or meet them for the first time by reading their stories together. Your librarian can recommend books for countries not on your list.

• Read with your child a book set in the country of your ancestors.

• Many bookstores carry classic picture books in foreign-language editions. Compare one with the English version and see how many foreign words you and your children recognize.

• Remember that not all "foreign" countries are on a map. Books can transport us to such strange places as Oz, the Land of Nod, Narnia, and Wonderland. How many imaginary countries can you and your child remember? Encourage your child to share with you a favorite story set in a fantasy land, then share one of your favorites.

Just Around the Corner

On our drive to school one morning, my eight-year-old son pointed at our neighborhood hardware store and said, "Mom, look! There's nothing there but an empty building. What happened?" Well . . . I was just as perplexed as he.

That unanswered question led to a guessing game in which we shared ideas about what went on in the buildings, houses, and parks we passed on our daily commute.

Here are some creative things to do the next time your family is out for a drive.

• Speculate about what goes on in a particular factory, warehouse, or office building. Some factories offer tours to the public. A family "field trip" to an automobile assembly plant or fish hatchery can be an unforgettable and educational experience.

• Before setting out on a trip across town, get a map and find your final destination. Mark out a route with a pen and encourage your child to follow along as you drive the car or ride public transportation. Is there another way to get from point "A" to point "B"?

• Plan an outing with your family to gain new experiences in your community. Decide what you would like to do, then map out your route together. If you typically drive your car, try going by foot, bicycle, or city bus. Fun things to do include watching boats on rivers, riding an elevator to a skyscraper's observation deck, watching a construction site in action, viewing airplanes landing and taking off, and participating in a special fair or festival (check newspapers for events and schedules).

Parents' Page

Tips for Solo Trips for Kids

Kids everywhere are on the go nowadays. For many young travelers, getting there may mean flying alone. If you're like most parents, it won't be easy sending a preteen or teenager on a solo journey for the first time. Here are tips to help ensure them a safe and enjoyable flight.

• Request from your airline a guide brochure designed for unaccompanied children. This outlines rules, regulations, and helpful safety tips.

• Make sure your child gets on the correct plane. During busy travel times, things can be confusing, especially if departure gates change at the last minute. Once the child boards, stay in the gate area until the plane is airborne.

• The adult meeting your child's plane should always call to check on the actual arrival time. Many flights are early, leaving kids to wait with the gate agent.

• Remind your child that it is OK to ask the flight attendant to review safety demonstrations for them. Airplane seatbelts may unfasten differently than automobile belts. Children may also request to be moved if seated next to someone who makes them uncomfortable. They should never give their address or phone number to another passenger.

• Pack an activity bag full of diversions —school backpacks are ideal. Include change for phone calls, and cash for headsets if you feel the on-board film is appropriate for your child.